The Lemonade Effect:
Thriving Amidst Adversity

Christopher Pickard

Introduction:

"Power of the Mind"

For years, I had grappled with a persistent sense of dissatisfaction regarding my financial situation. The belief that I wasn't making enough money weighed heavily on my mind, leading to anxiety and a constant comparison with others who appeared to be more financially successful. I felt trapped in a cycle of negativity, unable to break free from the shackles of this self-imposed mental prison. However, it was my determination to seek a healthier perspective that eventually set me on a path of positive change.

One of the most significant hurdles I had to overcome was the sense of workplace discrimination due to my race, specifically being Black. It was disheartening to experience skepticism and distrust from some colleagues and superiors simply because of the color of my skin. This discrimination cast a long shadow over my professional life, and it seemed like an insurmountable obstacle. Yet, I knew that letting these experiences define me was not an option; instead, I was determined to change the narrative. My journey towards transforming these negative thoughts and experiences began with introspection. I realized that I needed to confront my insecurities head-on. I discovered that my negative thoughts about money and workplace discrimination were deeply rooted in my own self-doubt and perceived inadequacies. I came to understand that these negative beliefs were

4

not a reflection of reality but rather a product of my mind's propensity to focus on the negative. Furthermore, I honed my skills and expertise, becoming an indispensable asset to my team. My dedication to excellence allowed me to demonstrate that my worth transcended the color of my skin. I focused on building trust through consistent, high-quality work, ultimately challenging the negative perceptions held by some colleagues and superiors.

A pivotal moment in my transformation occurred when I realized the importance of resilience and self-empowerment. I decided to confront the negativity that had taken residence in my mind and began practicing mindfulness and positive affirmations. Through meditation and self-reflection, I learned to let go of the past and focus on the present moment. I also started repeating positive affirmations daily, which gradually rewired my thought patterns. These practices enabled me to replace self-doubt with self-assurance and negativity with optimism.

On the physical front, I recognized that a healthy body was essential for maintaining a positive mindset. I incorporated regular exercise into my routine, not only for its physical benefits but also for its ability to reduce stress and improve mental clarity. My newfound commitment to physical well-being acted as a powerful complement to my mental transformation, reinforcing my belief that I was capable of achieving greatness.

In the quiet stillness of a beautiful summer morning, I found myself sitting on the edge of my bed, my mind a whirlwind of emotions. Three months ago, a devastating Achilles tendon tear had brought my world crashing down. The doctor's words had echoed in my ears, "This could take a year to heal, if not longer." But I was determined to prove them wrong, to find a way to heal faster, and to regain my life. Little did I know, my journey toward recovery would be as much about my mental state as it would be about physical healing. The first weeks were grueling. Crutches became my constant companions, and the simplest of tasks left me feeling hopeless. The pain was a constant reminder of my limitations. Yet, as time passed, I began to research alternative methods for recovery. One idea, in particular, caught my attention "the power of the placebo effect". I read about studies where patients had experienced significant improvements simply because they believed they were receiving treatment. It was as though the mind had the ability to influence the body's healing process. With this newfound knowledge, I decided to embark on a unique journey of recovery, one that would blend the power of positive thinking and the potential of placebo.

The first step was to change my mindset. Instead of dwelling on the pain and limitations, I focused on the progress I was making. I began visualizing myself walking, running with my daughter and playing basketball again. Every night, before falling asleep, I would close my eyes and see myself taking confident strides without crutches. Next, I delved into the world of supplements. I meticulously researched natural remedies known for their healing properties. Turmeric, known for its anti-inflammatory effects, became a staple in my diet. Collagen supplements were added to support tissue repair, and vitamin C along with Omega-3 was taken to boost the immune system. While these supplements may or may not have had a

8

direct impact, I believed in their potential to aid in my recovery. With newfound determination and a pocketful of supplements, I embarked on a daily routine that became my lifeline. I woke up each morning, staring at a picture of myself engaging in my favorite activities, reinforcing the belief that I would return to them. Then, I meticulously took my supplements, mentally affirming their healing powers. The weeks turned into months, and something miraculous began to happen. My physical therapist was astonished at the speed of my healing, and even I couldn't deny the noticeable changes. The pain subsided, and my mobility improved. It was as though my body was responding to the positive energy and belief I was channeling into it. Three months after that fateful diagnosis, I found myself on the verge of a breakthrough. I stand on two feet, unaided by crutches, running with my daughter and back playing basketball. The journey had been nothing short of remarkable, and I couldn't help but wonder how much of it was due to my changed mindset and the supplements.

Was it the power of placebo or a combination of factors? I may never know for sure. But what I did know was that I had defied the odds, shattered expectations, and found a renewed faith in the incredible connection between the mind and the body. My Achilles injury had become a catalyst for self-discovery and personal growth. It had taught me that the power of positivity and belief could be just as instrumental in healing as any medical treatment. As I continued my journey toward full recovery, I carried with me the invaluable lesson that our minds possess an extraordinary ability to shape our reality, turning the impossible into the possible.

Over time, the combination of therapy, financial empowerment, professional growth, mindfulness, physical well-being, and community engagement transformed my negative thoughts and experiences into sources of strength and resilience. I realized that my journey was not just about changing my own mindset but also about advocating for equality and inclusion.

In a world seemingly filled with stories of others living the good life, it's easy to succumb to feelings of inadequacy and envy. For a significant part of my life, I found myself trapped in the cycle of comparing my own circumstances to those of others, convinced that I was somehow missing out on the secret to happiness and success. However, my journey towards personal growth and fulfillment truly began when I made a conscious decision to shift my focus inward,

11

embracing a mindset that allowed me to discover new opportunities to make more money, and, equally importantly, to be positive and grateful for what I already possessed.

The pervasive influence of social media and the constant bombardment of curated images of success often left me feeling as though I were lagging behind in life. It was all too easy to believe that everyone else had unlocked the door to financial prosperity and a carefree existence, while I remained mired in mediocrity. But dwelling on these comparisons only served to deepen my discontent and hinder my progress. Recognizing that my obsession with others' perceived success was unproductive, I made a deliberate choice to redirect my energy towards self-improvement. I started by assessing my own strengths, interests, and skills, seeking out new opportunities that aligned with my passions.

12

This introspection allowed me to unearth untapped potential and explore avenues for personal and financial growth that I had previously overlooked.

Another pivotal moment in my journey was the realization that success is a deeply personal and subjective concept. It doesn't come with a one-size-fits-all formula, and what works for one person may not work for another. Armed with this insight, I began setting realistic, personalized goals that were tailored to my unique circumstances and aspirations. These goals provided a clear roadmap for my journey towards financial prosperity and personal fulfillment. While pursuing these objectives, I remained acutely aware of the importance of gratitude. It became evident to me that dwelling on what I didn't have was a self-defeating exercise. Instead, I started practicing gratitude daily, focusing on the

13

blessings and opportunities that already existed in my life. This shift in perspective allowed me to see the wealth of resources at my disposal and appreciate the value of what I had, rather than fixating on what I lacked. To augment my income, I embarked on a multifaceted approach that combined creativity, skill development, and entrepreneurship. I identified areas where my talents could be monetized, and took the initiative to market my skills and services. This proactive mindset not only increased my earning potential but also instilled a sense of empowerment and self-reliance. Additionally, I embraced the world of online learning and self-improvement. I sought out courses and resources that enabled me to acquire new skills and expand my knowledge base. This commitment to personal development not only enhanced my qualifications but also opened

14

doors to previously unexplored opportunities. I discovered that investing in myself was one of the most lucrative investments I could make.

Equally crucial to my transformation was the cultivation of a positive and resilient mindset. I understood that setbacks and challenges were an inherent part of any journey, but I refused to let them define me. Instead, I viewed these obstacles as opportunities for growth and learning. I began to practice mindfulness and meditation, which helped me navigate stress and adversity with grace and composure. This newfound mental fortitude not only improved my decision-making but also allowed me to maintain a sense of optimism even in the face of adversity. Moreover, I developed a habit of seeking out inspiration from those who had overcome their own challenges and achieved

15

their goals. Their stories served as a reminder that success was attainable, even when the path was fraught with obstacles. This sense of perspective bolstered my determination and provided me with the resilience to persevere in the pursuit of my dreams. In the midst of this transformative journey, I also began to contribute to the well-being of others. I realized that giving back to my community and supporting those in need brought a profound sense of fulfillment and purpose to my life. Whether it was through volunteering, mentoring, or simply offering a helping hand, I experienced the profound impact that acts of kindness could have on both myself and those around me.

In conclusion, my journey from battling negative thoughts about income, workplace discrimination and physically distressed to fostering a positive mindset, both mentally and physically, has been a transformative odyssey. Through introspection, professional growth, and mindfulness, I dismantled the walls of self-doubt and prejudice that had constrained me for so long. This journey is ongoing, but the progress I have made reminds me that change is possible, and positivity can prevail even in the face of adversity. My decision to shift my focus from others' apparent success to my own growth and fulfillment was a key moment in my life. By redirecting my energy towards self-improvement, embracing gratitude, and pursuing new opportunities, I not only increased my earning potential but also cultivated a deep sense of positivity and resilience. This journey taught me that true success is not measured by material possessions alone but by the richness of one's experiences and the impact one can have on the world. I am now not only grateful for what

17

I have but excited about the endless possibilities that lie ahead, knowing that my journey towards financial prosperity and personal fulfillment is an ongoing adventure filled with opportunities waiting to be explored.

In the journey of life, we all encounter moments that seem unbearably sour, like the bitter lemons that fate can throw our way. These moments might be challenges, setbacks, or unforeseen obstacles that threaten to derail our dreams and ambitions. But what if I told you that these lemons, no matter how sour, hold the potential to become something sweet, something refreshing, something transformative? This is the essence of "The Lemonade Effect." This book is not just another self-help guide; it's a roadmap to harnessing the power of Cognitive Behavioral

18

Therapy (CBT) to turn life's lemons into the most delicious lemonade you've ever tasted. CBT is a proven psychological approach that empowers individuals to understand and reframe their thought patterns, leading to healthier emotions and behaviors. It's a tool that can help you take control of your life, even when circumstances seem beyond your control. Using practical strategies for facing adversity head-on to the wisdom of those who have squeezed every drop of potential from their challenges, this book will equip you with the mental and emotional skills needed to transform adversity into opportunity. Whether you're grappling with personal setbacks, battling anxiety or depression, or simply seeking a more positive and productive outlook on life, the principles within these pages will guide you towards greater resilience and everlasting peace.

Chapter 1: Embracing the Sour Moments

In this chapter, we'll delve into the concept of obstacles and why they can seem overwhelming at times. We'll introduce the basics of Cognitive Behavioral Therapy (CBT) and how it can be a powerful tool for overcoming these challenges. You'll gain insights into how your thoughts, emotions, and behaviors are interconnected and how they impact your ability to face obstacles.

Life obstacles can feel overwhelming because they often challenge us, stretch our limits and force us to step out of our comfort zones. They can be unexpected, disruptive, or require significant effort to overcome. Additionally, when we face multiple obstacles at once or when they occur in a short period of time, it can make us feel overwhelmed and stressed. However, it's important to remember that obstacles are a natural part of life. They provide opportunities for growth, learning, and resilience.

- CBT teaches individuals to identify negative thoughts that contribute to feelings of overwhelm or stress. You can challenge these thoughts and replace them with more realistic and positive ones.

- CBT emphasizes the importance of self-awareness. By becoming aware of your thoughts, emotions, and behaviors in response to obstacles, you can better understand how they influence your well-being. This awareness allows you to make conscious choices and implement positive coping strategies.

- CBT helps individuals develop effective coping skills to deal with obstacles. These skills may include problem-solving, relaxation techniques, stress management, and assertiveness training. By acquiring these skills, you can navigate challenges more effectively and reduce the impact of obstacles on your well-being.

- CBT encourages individuals to set realistic and achievable goals. By breaking down larger obstacles into smaller, manageable steps, you can maintain motivation and track your progress. Celebrating small victories along the way reinforces a positive mindset and boosts resilience.

SCENARIO: Negative thought: "I'm going to fail at this task. I'm not good enough."

-Step 1: Identify the negative thoughts.

-Step 2: Evaluate the evidence. Challenge the negative thought by questioning its validity. Ask yourself if there is any evidence to support this thought or if it's just a result of self-doubt or negative thinking.

-Step 3: Find a more realistic positive thought. Generate an alternative thought that is more balanced and realistic. In this case, it

24

could be: "I may face challenges in this task, but I have skills and experience that can help me succeed. It's normal to feel uncertain, but I can learn and improve along the way."

-Step 4: Take action based on positive thought. Use the more realistic positive thought as a guide for your actions. Focus on implementing strategies and techniques that align with your positive belief and increase your chances of success.

To overcome obstacles effectively, it is essential to identify and understand them. Take the time to acknowledge and analyze the specific challenges you are facing. This self-awareness will enable you to develop appropriate strategies and find tailored solutions. By adopting a positive mindset and utilizing effective strategies, you can navigate through obstacles and come out stronger on the other side.

Chapter 2: The Power of Perspective

CBT focuses on identifying and challenging negative thought patterns that contribute to feelings of helplessness and despair. In this chapter, we'll explore common cognitive distortions and teach you how to recognize them in your own thinking. By becoming aware of these distortions, you'll take the first step towards changing your response to obstacles. Negative thoughts often manifest as self-critical statements. Some common indicators of negative thinking include:

1. Catastrophizing: Exaggerating the potential negative outcomes of a situation. An example of catastrophizing could be if someone receives a small criticism at work and immediately starts thinking that they're going to get fired, lose all their income, and end up homeless on the streets. They might start panicking and imagining the worst-case

scenario without considering more rational possibilities, such as the criticism being constructive feedback or not having significant consequences.

2. Overgeneralization: Drawing broad conclusions based on a single negative experience. An example of overgeneralization based on a single negative experience with a spouse might be when someone has an argument with their spouse and immediately concludes that their spouse is always unreasonable and never listens, even if it was just one isolated incident. This overgeneralization involves taking one negative event and applying it to the entire relationship, assuming that it represents a consistent pattern of behavior.

3. Personalization: Taking things personally and assuming blame for events beyond your control. For instance, if a person

blames themselves for their friend's bad mood, thinking, "It's my fault they're upset," when in reality, the friend's mood may have been influenced by various factors unrelated to them.

4. All-or-nothing thinking: Viewing situations as either completely good or completely bad, without considering the nuances in between. Imagine a student who believes, "If I don't get a perfect score on this test, I'm a total failure." This type of thinking disregards the possibility of doing well, but not perfectly, and can lead to excessive pressure and disappointment if they don't achieve a perfect score.

5. Filtering: Ignoring positive aspects and only focusing on the negative aspects of a situation. Suppose someone organizes a successful event where most attendees had a great time and provided positive feedback.

29

However, the organizer receives one negative comment from a participant. They then focus solely on that negative comment, dwelling on it and discounting all the positive feedback they received.

Scenario: "I can't believe I made that mistake at work. I'm such a failure."

This sounds like you're engaging in all-or-nothing thinking and putting too much blame on yourself for one mistake. Remember, everyone makes mistakes and it doesn't define your entire worth or capability. Instead of seeing this as a failure, think of it as an opportunity to learn and grow. Is there anything positive you can take away from this situation?

Once aware of these patterns, you can start identifying negative thoughts when they arise and consciously choose to challenge or reframe them. Overall, shifting your perspective allows for a broader view of a situation, which can lead to greater emotional well-being, problem-solving abilities, and personal growth.

Chapter 3: Resilience and Adaptation

Resilience is the remarkable ability of individuals and communities to bounce back from adversity, to withstand the harshest of obstacles, and to adapt in the face of overwhelming challenges. It is a fundamental trait of human nature, a testament to the courageous spirit that resides within us all. Throughout history, people have shown incredible resilience in the face of hardships, proving time and again that the human capacity to adapt and thrive in adversity knows no bounds. One of the key facets of resilience is the ability to confront adversity head-on, to acknowledge its presence, and to refuse to be defeated by it. When faced with daunting obstacles, resilient individuals do not succumb to despair. Instead, they muster the inner strength to confront their challenges with determination and resolve. This is illustrated in the stories of countless individuals who have faced life-altering events such as illness, loss, or natural disasters and have emerged from these trials stronger and more resilient than ever.

Resilience also entails the capacity to adapt and pivot in response to changing circumstances. Life rarely unfolds as planned, and obstacles are an inevitable part of the journey. Resilient individuals do not severe to a predetermined path but instead remain flexible and open to new possibilities. They embrace change as an opportunity for growth and transformation, rather than a setback. This adaptability enables them to navigate the twists and turns of life with grace. Moreover, resilience is closely tied to the concept of emotional fortitude. It involves the ability to regulate one's emotions in the face of adversity, to remain composed under pressure, and to find solace in the midst of chaos. This emotional resilience allows individuals to process their experiences and find meaning in even the most challenging situations. It enables them to connect with others, seeking support and providing it in return, thus creating a web of resilience that extends far beyond themselves.

In times of hardship, individuals draw strength from the bonds they share with others. Communities that come together in times of crisis exemplify the collective resilience that can emerge when people unite with a shared sense of purpose and solidarity. Whether it's a neighborhood rallying to rebuild after a disaster or a group of friends providing support to someone in need, these connections form the base of resilience.

Moreover, resilience is a skill that involves building a toolkit of coping strategies, pursuing a growth mindset, and seeking out resources and support when needed.

Here are 11 key steps to adapt and reconstruct negative thought patterns:

Acceptance of Reality: **Acknowledge that tough times are a part of life. Acceptance doesn't mean resignation but understanding that change is inevitable.**

Mindset Shift: **Cultivate a growth mindset. See challenges as opportunities for growth and learning rather than impossible obstacles.**

Emotional Regulation: **Learn to manage your emotions. This includes recognizing and accepting your feelings without judgment and finding healthy ways to express them.**

Set Realistic Goals: **Break down your long-term goals into smaller, achievable steps.**

This can make progress feel more attainable and less overwhelming.

Flexibility and Adaptability: Be open to change and adapt as needed. Sometimes, the ability to pivot and adjust your plans is crucial in tough times.

Seek Support: Lean on your support network. Share your concerns and seek advice or emotional support from friends, family, or mentors.

Self-Care: Prioritize self-care, including physical health, mental well-being, and relaxation techniques like meditation or deep breathing.

Problem-Solving Skills: Develop problem-solving skills to address challenges effectively. Identify the issue, brainstorm solutions, and take action.

Resilience Building: Continuously work on building resilience through practices like gratitude, positive self-talk, and maintaining a sense of purpose.

Learn from Setbacks: View setbacks as opportunities to learn and grow stronger. Analyze what went wrong and apply those lessons to future endeavors.

Stay Optimistic: Maintain a hopeful outlook. Optimism can help you navigate tough times with a positive attitude.

In conclusion, resilience is a remarkable human quality that empowers individuals and communities to confront and adapt to hard obstacles. It is characterized by determination to face adversity head-on, an ability to adapt and pivot in response to changing circumstances, and the power of community and social support. Resilience is a testament to the human spirit's ability to endure and emerge stronger, no matter the obstacles that lie in its path.

Chapter 4: Finding the Sweet Spots

CBT doesn't stop at changing your thoughts; it also addresses emotions and behaviors. Finding the sweet spot within ourselves amidst the myriad negative obstacles that life throws our way is a journey as intricate and profound as the human experience itself. It's a quest that unfolds not in a single sweeping revelation, but in the subtle interplay of resilience, self-discovery, and the relentless pursuit of balance. Life, by its very nature, is fraught with challenges. From the daily struggles that punctuate our existence to the seismic shifts that can upend our entire world, obstacles are woven into the fabric of our journey. These obstacles, both external and internal, often manifest in the form of self-doubt, fear, adversity, and uncertainty. They loom large, casting shadows over our aspirations and dreams. Yet, it's within the context of these very shadows that the sweet spot beckons us.

The first step in this quest is the recognition that negativity is an intrinsic part of life. It's acknowledging that without darkness, there can be no appreciation of light. In facing adversity, we begin to recognize the contours of our own strengths and weaknesses. The first glimmer of the sweet spot emerges when we understand that these obstacles are not merely roadblocks but stepping stones toward self-discovery.

Self-awareness is the compass that guides us on this journey. To find the sweet spot, we must delve into the depths of our being, peeling back the layers of conditioning and societal expectations to reveal the core of our authentic selves. It's in this process of self-discovery that we uncover our unique talents, passions, and purposes. These are the gifts that, when nurtured and channeled, become the keys to unlocking the sweet spot within.

Yet, the path to self-discovery is not without its own obstacles. Negative self-talk, self-limiting beliefs, and the fear of vulnerability can be formidable adversaries. They can obscure our view of the sweet spot, clouding our judgment and stifling our growth. Confronting these inner demons, dismantling their influence, is a heroic undertaking in itself. It requires the cultivation of self compassion, the audacity to challenge our own narratives, and the resilience to persevere in the face of self-doubt.

As we navigate this labyrinthine terrain of the self, we come to understand that the sweet spot is not a fixed point but a dynamic equilibrium. It's not a destination but a state of being that ebbs and flows with the rhythms of our lives. Just as a tightrope walker maintains balance through constant adjustments, so too must we recalibrate our inner equilibrium as circumstances evolve. This adaptability is the essence of resilience, the ability to bounce back from setbacks and find the sweet spot anew.

Resilience, however, is not a solitary endeavor. It thrives in the soil of community and connection. In the face of negative obstacles, seeking support and guidance from mentors, friends, and loved ones can be a lifeline. The sweet spot is often illuminated by the wisdom and encouragement of those who have walked similar paths. Their insights can serve as beacons, guiding us through the darkest of times.

Yet, the sweet spot is not solely about personal growth; it's also about contribution. Finding fulfillment in the midst of obstacles is intrinsically linked to how we impact the world

43

around us. Our unique gifts and passions, uncovered through self-discovery, find their fullest expression when we use them to uplift others. In this way, the sweet spot becomes a nexus of purpose, where our individual journeys intersect with the greater tapestry of humanity.

Negativity, in all its forms, becomes a crucible through which we refine our character and deepen our empathy. It challenges us to summon our inner strength, creativity, and resilience. It compels us to question, adapt, and grow. In this sense, the very obstacles that obscure the sweet spot also serve as catalysts for its revelation.

As we navigate this intricate terrain, let us remember that the sweet spot is not a destination but a continuous voyage, a perpetual balancing act. It's the art of embracing life's obstacles as opportunities, of finding joy in the face of adversity, and of realizing that within us, there exists a wellspring of strength and resilience waiting to be tapped. In this ongoing quest, we discover that the sweet spot is not elusive; it is, in fact, the very essence of our humanity, waiting to be uncovered and celebrated in each moment of our lives.

In the final analysis, finding the sweet spot within ourselves between negative obstacles in life is not a static achievement but a dynamic process. It's a dance between self-awareness and self-acceptance, between resilience and adaptability, between personal growth and collective contribution. It's a journey that requires courage, vulnerability, and unwavering faith in the capacity of the human spirit to transcend adversity.

Chapter 5: Turning Ideas into Action

"Lemons to Lemonade"

Now, let's focus on turning your newfound perspective and resilience into concrete actions. You'll learn how to set meaningful goals, develop plans, and take steps towards making positive changes in your life, no matter the obstacles. Setting Meaningful Goals, Developing Plans, and Overcoming Obstacles.

The pursuit of positive change is a fundamental aspect of human existence. Whether it's achieving personal growth, professional success, or simply leading a more fulfilling life, setting meaningful goals and taking deliberate steps towards them is essential. However, the journey towards positive change is often riddled with obstacles and challenges that can make one lose sight of their goals. In this essay, we will explore the process of setting meaningful goals, developing effective plans, and overcoming obstacles to create a roadmap for achieving positive changes in life.

I. Setting Meaningful Goals: The first step on the path to positive change is setting meaningful goals. These goals act as guiding stars, providing direction and purpose to our actions. Meaningful goals should possess several key characteristics:

1. Clarity: Goals should be specific and well-defined. Ambiguity can lead to confusion and hinder progress. For instance, instead of setting a vague goal like "get in shape," one could set a clear goal like "lose 20 pounds in six months by following a regular exercise routine and a healthy diet."

2. Relevance: Goals should align with your values and aspirations. Pursuing goals that resonate with your inner desires and beliefs will foster greater motivation and commitment.

3. Achievability: While it's important to dream big, setting unrealistic goals can lead to frustration and demotivation. Goals should be challenging but attainable with effort and dedication.

4. Time-Bound: Establishing a timeframe for achieving goals creates a sense of urgency and accountability. This helps prevent procrastination and maintains focus.

5. Measurable: Goals should be quantifiable to track progress effectively. This might involve tracking metrics like weight, income, or the number of hours spent on a particular task.

II. Developing Plans: Setting meaningful goals is only the beginning; the next step is to develop comprehensive plans to achieve them. Planning is the bridge between aspirations and actions. Here are essential components of effective planning:

49

1. Break Goals into Smaller Steps: **Large goals can be overwhelming. Breaking them into smaller, manageable steps makes them less daunting and easier to approach. For example, if your goal is to start a successful business, the smaller steps might include market research, business plan development, and securing funding.**

2. Create a Timeline: **Develop a timeline that outlines when each step of your plan will be completed. This establishes a sense of structure and helps in tracking progress. Be realistic in your timeline to avoid unnecessary pressure.**

3. Allocate Resources: **Identify the resources you will need to achieve your goals, whether it's time, money, skills, or support from others. Ensure you have access to these resources or create a plan to acquire them.**

50

4. Adaptability: Life is unpredictable, and obstacles may arise unexpectedly. Build flexibility into your plans to accommodate changes and setbacks. This adaptability will prevent discouragement when things don't go as expected.

5. Visualize Success: Visualization is a powerful tool for motivation. Regularly picture yourself achieving your goals. This can boost confidence and reinforce your commitment to the plan.

III. Taking Steps towards Positive Change: Once you've set meaningful goals and developed plans, the next crucial step is taking action. Positive change does not happen without deliberate effort and persistence. Here's how to turn your plans into action:

1. Prioritize and Focus: With a clear plan in hand, prioritize your tasks and focus on

completing them one at a time. Multitasking can lead to burnout and reduced efficiency.

2. Consistency: Consistency is key to making progress. Establish daily or weekly routines that align with your goals. Small, consistent actions add up over time.

3. Seek Support and Accountability: Share your goals with friends, family, or a mentor who can provide support and hold you accountable. Their encouragement can be invaluable during challenging times.

4. Learn from Failure: Setbacks and failures are inevitable. Instead of viewing them negatively, see them as opportunities for growth and learning. Analyze what went wrong, adjust your plans if necessary, and keep moving forward.

IV. Overcoming Obstacles: Obstacles are an inherent part of any journey towards positive change. The ability to overcome these

52

obstacles is often what separates successful goal achievers from those who give up. Here are strategies to tackle common obstacles:

1. Fear and Self-Doubt: Self-doubt and fear of failure can be paralyzing. Counteract these feelings by focusing on your strengths, past successes, and the progress you've already made. Surround yourself with a positive and supportive environment.

2. Procrastination: Procrastination is a common roadblock. Combat it by breaking tasks into smaller, more manageable pieces, setting deadlines, and eliminating distractions.

3. Lack of Motivation: Motivation can wane over time. Rekindle your motivation by reminding yourself why your goals are meaningful to you, revisiting your initial enthusiasm, or seeking inspiration from others who have achieved similar goals.

4. Time Constraints: **Many individuals struggle with time constraints due to work, family, or other commitments. To overcome this obstacle, optimize your time management skills, delegate tasks when possible, and make your goals a priority.**

5. Financial Constraints: **If your goals require financial resources you don't currently possess, explore options like budgeting, saving, seeking funding, or finding cost-effective alternatives.**

The path to positive change is a challenging but rewarding journey. By setting meaningful goals, developing effective plans, taking consistent action, and overcoming obstacles, individuals can achieve personal growth, professional success, and a more fulfilling life. Remember that change is a process, and setbacks are a part of it. Stay resilient, adapt to challenges, and continue progressing towards your goals. In the end, the pursuit of positive change is not just about reaching a destination; it's about the transformation that occurs along the way.

Chapter 6: Zest for Success

In the final moments of our journey through these pages, I want you to pause and reflect on the incredible capacity of the human spirit. We embarked on this voyage together to explore the art of thriving amidst adversity, and now, as we reach the end, it's time to embrace the profound lessons we've learned. Adversity is an inevitable part of life. It is the storm that tests the strength of our sails, the darkness that forces us to seek the light within ourselves. It can take many forms - personal loss, financial hardship, health crises, or societal upheaval - but it is how we respond to adversity that defines us.

Thriving in the face of adversity is not about escaping hardship, nor is it about pretending that difficulties don't exist. It's about acknowledging the challenges, embracing them as opportunities for growth, and finding the strength within to transcend them.

One of the recurring themes throughout this book has been the power of perspective. Your outlook on life, the lens through which you view the world, can be your greatest asset or your most formidable obstacle. Those who thrive amidst adversity have a remarkable ability to shift their perspective, to see the silver linings in even the darkest of clouds.

In every story, there is a moment when the protagonist decides not to be defined by their circumstances but to define their circumstances. They chose to be the authors of their own narratives, writing tales of resilience, courage, and transformation. Adversity, in all its forms, can be a catalyst for personal growth and positive change. But thriving amidst adversity is not a solitary endeavor. It often requires the support and encouragement of

58

others. Just as we draw inspiration from the stories of those who have overcome adversity, we too can inspire and uplift those around us. Our actions and words have the power to be a beacon of hope for someone navigating their own storm.

I encourage you to carry forward the wisdom you've gained. When faced with adversity, remember that you have the inner strength to weather the storm. Embrace challenges as opportunities for growth, and never underestimate the power of your perspective to shape your reality. Life will undoubtedly continue to present its challenges, but you are equipped with the tools to not only survive but thrive amidst adversity. The path may be rocky at times, but with determination, resilience, and a positive outlook, you can navigate it with grace and emerge on the other side stronger than you ever imagined. In the words of Maya Angelou, "You may encounter many defeats, but you must not be defeated. In fact, it may be necessary to encounter the defeats so you can know who you are, what you can rise from, and how you can still come out of it."

So, my friend, as you turn the final page of this book, know that your journey is far from over. Embrace the challenges that come your way as opportunities for growth and transformation. Thrive amidst adversity, and in doing so, inspire others to do the same.

Thank you for joining me on this exploration of the human spirit's remarkable ability to not only endure but to triumph over adversity. May your life be filled with resilience, courage, and the unwavering belief that you have the power to thrive, no matter what challenges lie ahead.

NOTES

THINK - ACT - BE

_____
_____
_____
_____
_____
_____
_____
_____
_____
_____
_____
_____
_____
_____
_____
_____

LET OF OF:

EGO

ENTITLEMENT

RESENTMENT

HATE

DOUBT

HOLD ON TO:

HOPE

GRATITUDE

OPTIMISM

CURIOSITY

LOVE

TODAY IS THE DAY YOU STOP BEING AFRAID OF WHAT CAN GO WRONG IN YOUR LIFE & START PUTTING YOUR POSITIVE ENERGY TOWARDS ALL THAT CAN GO RIGHT!

<u>NEVER:</u>

EXPECT

DEMAND

ASSUME

<u>KNOW:</u>

YOUR LIMITS

WHAT YOU DON'T KNOW

YOUR POTENTIAL

<u>DON'T:</u>

GET NEGATIVE

GET JEALOUS

WORRY ABOUT WHAT OTHERS

ARE DOING

REPEAT X10

I AM SO HAPPY AND GRATEFUL,THAT MONEY COMES TO ME IN INCREASING QUANTITIES, THROUGH MULTIPLE SOURCES, ON A CONTINUOUS BASIS.

ADVICE FOR ALL:

1. READ AND WRITE MORE

2. STAY HEALTHY

3. NETWORKING IS ABOUT GIVING

4. PRACTICE PUBLIC SPEAKING

5. STAY TEACHABLE

6. FIND A MENTOR

7. KEEP IN TOUCH WITH FRIENDS

8. YOU ARE NOT YOUR JOB

9. KNOW WHEN TO LEAVE

10. DON'T SPEND WHAT YOU DON'T HAVE

Made in the USA
Monee, IL
13 October 2023

44529687R00044